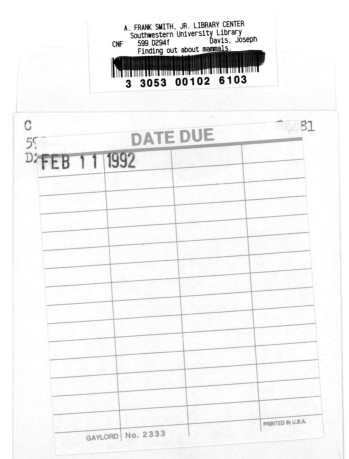

C   81
59
D2 FEB 11 1992

DATE DUE

GAYLORD | No. 2333   PRINTED IN U.S.A.

FINDING OUT ABOUT MAMMALS

By

Joseph A. Davis, Jr.

Curator of Mammals

New York Zoological Park

Illustrated by
Lloyd Sanford

FINDING-OUT BOOKS

HOME LIBRARY PRESS

New York, N. Y.

CONTENTS

EIGHT-PAGE COLOR INSERT

CAMOUFLAGE   FEET   SENSES   COLOR   DEFENSE
HORNS AND ANTLERS   LIFE IN THE WATER

ORDERS AND FAMILIES OF MAMMALS

Because limits of space in this book made it impossible to include all of the names of the Orders of mammals in the text, the following list of Orders* and Families** mentioned in this book is given below.

MONOTREMATA Egg-laying Mammals
Ornithorhynchidae Platypus
Tachyglossidae Echidnas

MARSUPIALIA Pouched Mammals
Peramelidae Bandicoots
Phalangeridae Phalangers, Marsupial
          "mice," "wolf," etc.
Phascolomidae Wombats
Macropodidae Kangaroos
Didelphiidae Opossums

INSECTIVORA Insect-eaters
Solenodontidae Solenodons
Tenrecidae Tenrecs
Chrysochloridae Golden Moles
Erinaceidae Hedgehogs
Macroscelididae Elephant Shrews
Soricidae Shrews
Talpidae Moles

DERMOPTERA
Cynocephalidae Flying "Lemurs"

CHIROPTERA Bats
Pteropodidae Flying "Foxes"
Microchiroptera All the families
          of small bats

PRIMATES Primates
Tupaiidae Tree-shrews
Lemuridae Lemurs
Indriidae Indris
Daubentoniidae Aye-aye
Lorisidae Pottos, Lorises
          and Galagos
Tarsiidae Tarsiers
Callithricidae Marmosets
Cebidae New World Monkeys
Cercopithecidae Old World Monkeys
Pongidae Great Apes

EDENTATA "Toothless" Mammals
Myrmecophagidae Anteaters
Bradypodidae Sloths
Dasypodidae Armadillos

PHOLIDOTA Scaly Mammals
Manidae Pangolins

LAGOMORPHA Rabbits, Hares and Pikas
Leporidae Rabbits and Hares
Ochotonidae Pikas

RODENTIA Gnawing Mammals
Aplodontidae Sewellel
Sciuridae Squirrels
Geomyidae Pocket Gophers
Heteromyidae Pocket Mice, Kangaroo Rats, etc.
Castoridae Beavers

Cricetidae Hamster Family (Rats, Mice, etc.)
Pedetidae Springhaas
Muridae Old World Mice and Rats
Zapodidae Jumping Mice
Dipodidae Jerboas
Histricidae Old World Porcupines
Erethizontidae New World Porcupines
Caviidae Cavies
Hydrochoeridae Capybara
Dinomyidae Pacarana

CETACEA Whales and Porpoises
Platanistidae River Dolphins
Physeteridae Sperm Whales
Monodontidae Narwhal and Beluga
Delphinidae Dolphins
Phocaenidae Porpoises
Balaenopteridae Finback Whales
Balaenidae Right Whales

CARNIVORA Meat-Eaters
Canidae Dogs, Wolves and Foxes
Ursidae Bears
Procyonidae Raccoon Family
Mustelidae Weasel Family
Viverridae Civet Family
Hyaenidae Hyenas
Felidae Cats
Phocidae Earless Seals
Otariidae Eared, or Fur Seals
Odobaenidae Walrus

TUBULIDENTATA Tube-toothed Mammals
Orycteropodidae Aardvark

PROBOSCIDEA Trunked Mammals
Elephantidae Elephants

HYDRACOIDEA Hyraxes
Procaviidae Hyraxes

SIRENIA Sea Cows
Manatidae Manatee
Dugongidae Dugong

PERISSODACTYLA Odd-toed Hoofed Mammals
Equidae Horses
Tapiridae Tapirs
Rhinocerotidae Rhinoceroses

ARTIODACTYLA Even-toed Hoofed Mammals
Suidae Pigs
Tayassuidae Peccaries
Hippopotamidae Hippopotamuses
Camelidae Camels, Llama, Guanaco, Vicuna
Tragulidae Chevrotains
Cervidae Deer
Giraffidae Giraffe, Okapi
Antilocapridae Pronghorn
Bovidae Cattle, Goats, Sheep, Antelopes

*Orders are printed in black-face capital letters.
**Families are printed in italic letters and the English equivalents are shown in regular print.

ACKNOWLEDGEMENTS

Photographs for the eight-page color insert WAYS OF LIFE, were supplied by the following:

J. A. Davis: Allegheny Packrat, Florida Packrat, Muskox, Tree Kangaroo (endpaper)

Russ Kinne: Pangolin, Rhinoceros, Caribou, Giraffe, Bighorn Sheep, Canada Porcupine, Coati, Black-shouldered Opossum, Nyala, Mandrill, Fennec, Bushbaby, Jaguarundis, Otter, Polar Bear, California Sea Lion, Whitetail Deer, Clouded Leopard, Lion, Bottle-nosed Dolphin, Zebra, Harp Seal, River Otter

The New York Zoological Park: Long-Snouted Dik-Dik (cover), Leopard in tree (endpaper)

Insert Design by **Phyllis Stevens**

Introduction

IF YOU ASK someone to give you the name of an animal, chances are that he will name a mammal, for to most of us "mammal" and "animal" are synonymous. Actually, birds, reptiles and amphibians, fishes, insects—even the microscopic protozoans—are animals. Mammals are only one kind, but they are so familiar to us that they are usually uppermost in our minds. We are mammals ourselves, and our history is closely bound to other members of this group.

Mammals are vertebrates; that is, they belong to a larger group of animals that have a jointed, bony column down the back, which helps support the body and protect the spinal chord. The spinal chord is enlarged at the front end to form a very complex brain, which not only controls the regular, "automatic" body functions such as breathing, but allows the vertebrate to perform a greater number of voluntary acts, and to learn from experience to a far greater degree than invertebrates can. The most complex vertebrate brains are found in mammals, and they are therefore more intelligent than any other kind of animal.

Many things set mammals apart from other animals; mammals alone have hair (although it may be present in whales as only a few bristles around the mouth, or even be completely lost before birth). Females feed their young with milk secreted from mammary glands in the skin. The lower jaw, made of many small bones in reptiles, is reduced to a single bone in mammals, and the teeth are modified in most mammals to perform different tasks, such as cutting, slashing, and grinding. The red blood cells, unlike those of other animals, are flat and disc-shaped (except in the camel family, where they are oval), and lose their nuclei during formation, which probably allows the cells to carry more oxygen to other cells of the body. These are but a few of the ways in which mammals have become the most efficient, and dominant form of life on Earth.

In this book we will look at the mammals by family. The word, in this sense means a series of species that are more closely related to one another, through evolution, than to any others. Some families contain only one species, which is so unlike other mammals that it does not fit into any other family. Some families are large, but all their members look pretty much alike, as the cat family, for example. Other families have members whose relationship is shown by internal structure, and which are very unlike externally, as the dasyurids (note that the scientific name of a family ends with the suffix -idae, and that in English the -ae is dropped.)

Two very well known orders, the rodents and the bats, have so many families that there isn't space in this book to list all of them. We have picked both the commonest and the most unusual in this case.

The relationships of mammals are not yet completely known, and from time to time the species in two or more families may be grouped together into one, or one family may be split into two or more, as scientific knowledge advances. This is why, if you read other books about mammals you may find differences as to grouping. The only really natural animal group is the species, and all the other categories (genus, family, order) are man-made groupings of species, by zoologists who are trying to uncover the course of evolution.

RHESUS MONKEY

SHORT-BEAKED ECHIDNA

LONG-BEAKED ECHIDNA

Egg-Laying Mammals

THE PLATYPUS and the two kinds of echidnas are all that remain of a very early group of mammals that were closely related to the reptiles. Oddly enough, none of the characteristics that show this primitiveness are visible externally, for these animals have become so modified for their special ways of life that they probably look very different from their early ancestors, thought to have been shrew-like in appearance. The bones of the shoulders look more like those of reptiles than mammals, and the monotremes reproduce by laying eggs, as reptiles do, but the platypus and echidnas nurse their young with milk.

Platypus (ORNITHORHYNCHIDAE)

The platypus of Australia, a small animal, about two feet long, is most notable for its grayish, rubbery "bill," shaped like that of a duck. Unlike a duck's bill, the platypus's snout contains an abundance of nerve endings, is very sensitive, and is used to locate crayfish and other aquatic animals on which the platypus feeds. All four feet of the platypus are webbed.

Echidnas (TACHYGLOSSIDAE)

The echidnas or spiny anteaters, of Australia and New Guinea look not at all like the platypus, and form their own family. They are toothless, long snouted creatures well adapted for both burrowing and digging into the nests of ants and termites. The claws of the fore feet are very large and strong. The upper surface of echidnas is protected by hedgehog-like quills or spines, which hide the coat of hair in most species. Echidnas, like the platypus, lay eggs, but incubate them in a small pouch on the mother's abdomen.

PLATYPUS

7

Pouched Mammals

THE MARSUPIALS are more advanced than the monotremes, but have many characteristics that are less efficient than "typical" mammals. The young are born in a far less developed state than, for example, those of a dog or a monkey. Female marsupials have a pouch into which the young crawl after birth, and where they continue to develop for several months. (A few kinds, like the mouse opossums do not have pouches.) Marsupials of a few kinds are found in Central and South America (one species occurs in North America, too), but it is in Australia that they have come into their own. Pouched mammals migrated to Australia before it became separated from Asia, and before other, higher mammals arrived, so that when that continent was cut off from the mainland, the marsupials had it all to themselves. With no competition, they multiplied and evolved into many kinds, adapted for many different ways of life. So closely do some of these resemble the "typical" mammals, that early naturalists did not recognize marsupials as a distinct order. Within one family, the Dasyuridae, are

DASYURES
"NATIVE CAT"

BANDED ANTEATER

TASMANIAN WOLF

TASMANIAN DEVIL

YELLOW-FOOTED
MARSUPIAL MOUSE

AUSTRALIAN POSSUM

KOALA

found marsupial "mice," a marsupial "wolf," a marsupial "anteater," the dasyures, or "native cats," and the Tasmanian Devil, which resembles a badger. Another family is represented by a marsupial "mole."

Bandicoots (PERAMELIDAE)

The bandicoot family contains a number of rodent-like animals that vary from vegetarians to flesh-eaters, though most are omnivorous.

Phalanger Family

Another different - looking group of species makes up the Phalanger family. Most of these are called possums, although they are only distantly related to the American, or true possums. The largest members of the family are the slow moving cuscuses, which closely resemble kinkajous, and have similar habits. Their close relatives, the gliders, mostly look and act like flying squirrels. The most familiar member of the family is the koala, which looks like a bear, but has habits like a sloth, and eats only the leaves of the eucalyptus trees.

Wombats (PHASCOLOMIDAE)

The common wombat and hairy-nosed wombat are marsupial counterparts of the woodchucks. They are strict vegetarians and their teeth resemble those of rodents. They are nocturnal, and spend the day in burrows.

WOMBAT

9

RAT KANGAROO

TREE KANGAROO

RED KANGAROO

Kangaroos (MACROPODIDAE)

Most members of the kangaroo family are alike in appearance. They have short forefeet and extremely strong, large hind feet with one toe much larger than the others. All have long, heavy tails used as a prop when they sit up, and as a balancing organ while they hop. When walking slowly kangaroos use all four feet, but in a hurry, they move in great bounds on the hind feet only. Small species are called wallabies, and medium sized species are called wallaroos. Smaller than the wallabies are the rat-kangaroos, whose diet includes insects as well as plants. The hind legs of rat-kangaroos are not as extremely developed as in their larger cousins. An odd offshoot of this family is the tree kangaroo, whose hind feet are comparatively short and broad, and adapted for life in the branches of trees. Kangaroos are vegetarians.

Opossums (DIDELPHIIDAE)

The true opossums (or possums) are inhabitants of the New World. One species, the Virginia Opossum is common from the United States, to the tropics of South America. Other members of this family are all tropical, and include the tiny mouse opossum and the four-eyed opossum. All of the American opossums eat a variety of foods. The Yapok, or water opossum is a strikingly marked animal with webbed feet; its diet includes fish.

VIRGINIA OPOSSUM

Placental Mammals

HAITIAN SOLENODON

THESE ARE the most highly developed of mammals, and are represented by the most species. The developing young is nourished within the mother's body by a contact of its blood system with the mother's, through a membranous structure called the placenta. Placental mammals develop longer and more completely before birth. Most are born naked and helpless, but a few, like the hares, are furred and able to move about at birth, or shortly after.

"Insect-Eaters"

One of the most primitive known orders of mammals, most species feed heavily, if not exclusively, on insects and other small invertebrates. Their teeth are many and sharp, with edges adapted to cut through the hard shells of their prey.

COMMON TENREC

Solenodons (SOLENODONTIDAE)

Only two species form this family, and one of these, the Cuban Solenodon, may already be extinct. On the island of Haiti, the Haitian Solenodon, about the size of a large rat, still exists in some numbers. Solenodons are nocturnal, eat a variety of animal food, and probably some vegetable matter.

Tenrecs (TENRECIDAE)

The tenrecs are found only on the island of Madagascar, where there are several species. The Common Tenrec, one of the most primitive of the insectivores, is nocturnal and chiefly insectivorous. Its body is covered with an unkempt coat of coarse, bristly hair.

LONG-EARED HEDGEHOG

surface is clothed in a dense coat of sharp spines. When alarmed, hedgehogs double up into a prickly ball, protecting their soft undersides. Their diet is much more varied than most insectivores and includes small animals and fruit.

Elephant "Shrews"
(MACROSCELIDIDAE)

This family contains some of the most unusual looking creatures in the order. The best known species, the Common Elephant Shrew, has a long, tapering flexible snout, which it pokes into small spaces where its insect prey hides.

Golden Moles
(CHRYSOCHLORIDAE)

The several members of this family, all African, spend their lives burrowing, like the true moles, eating worms and other invertebrates. Their fur is a beautiful golden color, and their front feet bear two prominent, stout claws. Like the true moles, their eyes are covered by skin and they lack external ears.

Shrews (SORICIDAE)

Shrews are small insectivores that look like mice with long, pointed snouts. They have a great many teeth, adapted for capturing

ELEPHANT SHREW

Hedgehogs (ERINACEIDAE)

The hedgehogs are Old-World animals with sharp, pointed snouts and fat bodies whose upper

and chewing the hard bodies of insects and other arthropods. Shrews are among the smallest of mammals; the Pigmy Shrew of North America is scarcely more than two inches long, including the tail, and often weighs less than a dime. One of the rarest shrews in the United States, the Long-tailed Shrew is restricted to very cold, damp habitats, while another species, the Masked Shrew, occurs over an area of about two million square miles in the northern half of North America, in almost every kind of habitat except desert. The water shrews of North America, Europe and Asia swim well, diving to the bottoms of streams and

WATER-SHREW

ponds to capture their invertebrate prey. Although their tiny feet are not webbed, rows of bristles on the sides of the feet serve the same purpose. Shrews use up such great amounts of energy, because they are so small, that they must eat much more frequently than most mammals. They rest a great deal, but often consume more than their own weight in food every day.

PIGMY SHREW

SHORT-TAILED SHREW

STAR-NOSED MOLE

Moles (TALPIDAE)

Moles are stocky burrowing insectivores with forefeet enlarged and shovel-like. They spend most of their lives underground. The Star-nosed Mole has twenty-two fleshy projections on the tip of its snout, which are sensitive to touch and probably help to locate the earthworms and other invertebrates upon which it preys. The Desman, or Water Mole of Europe and Asia is a large, otter-like insectivore, about 18 inches long. The fur of moles is short and plushy, and does not become ruffled when rubbed the wrong way. A mole can back out of a narrow tunnel without difficulty.

COLUGO

Flying "Lemurs," Or Colugos

O NLY ONE family exists, containing two species, limited to south-east Asia and nearby islands. While colugos have lemur-like heads, they are not closely related to these primates, and are so peculiar that they stand alone in their own order. Neither do they fly, but rather glide like the flying squirrels. The larger of the two species is about a foot and a half long, with a parachute-like membrane that stretches from the neck to the tail enclosing the limbs, turning the animal into a living kite. When at rest, the colugo's elastic membrane contracts and folds partly out of the way.

Bats

L OOK AT the wing of a bat and the gliding membrane of a colugo. They are similar, except the bat's membrane does not extend between the toes of its hind foot. Notice, too, that the same bones are found in both forelimbs, and that these are the same bones that you have in your hand and arm. The colugo's hand, although it is webbed, is probably of little importance in gliding because it is so small, but the hand of a bat has grown so huge that it forms the main part of the wing.

Although bats are the only order of mammals to attain true flight, they have been so successful that there are more species in the order than in any other except for the rodents. Bats are found throughout the world except in the extreme polar regions, but are most numerous in the tropics. Bats fall into two main groups, called Megachiroptera ("large bats") and Microchiroptera ("small bats").

Flying Foxes (PTEROPIDAE)

Here are the largest of all bats, the flying foxes, some species of which have wingspans over five feet, but the family also contains the tiny blossom bats, which feed on nectar, like hummingbirds. Except for the blossom bats members of this family are all fruit eaters. The Megachiroptera have large eyes and can fly by sight.

FLYING FOX

Small Bats

WHILE ALL of the Megachiroptera belong to the same family, this second subdivision of the bats contains about sixteen families. Because there are so many families, and the bats in them have much the same habits we will group them here, not by family, but by food habits.

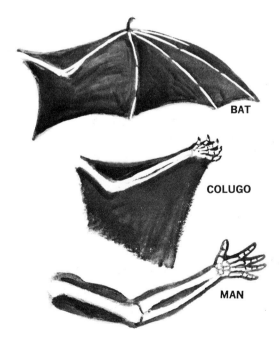

BAT

COLUGO

MAN

Most of the small bats feed exclusively on insects, which they capture in the air (a few species can find insects on the ground). Various species have adopted other diets. Like the flying foxes of the Old World, smaller bats in the New World tropics, have also taken to a diet of fruit. Other small bats, the Long-tongued Bat, for example, like the Old World blossom bats, have become, in a sense, hummingbirds of the night, and can hover in front of flowers, extending their long, bristle-tipped tongues deep within to feed on pollen and nectar. Like humming-

colder regions some spend the winter asleep in them. Other bats are partial to hollow trees, and still others hang out in the open. The Red Bat leaves North America in the fall and migrates across the Gulf of Mexico to South America.

How can bats fly in the dark and catch insects without crashing headlong into obstacles? Most

birds, they help to spread pollen from one flower to another. In the Gulf of Mexico live bats which dine on fish which they catch by raking the water surface with their huge hind feet.

The Spear-nosed Bat, which belongs to the fruit-eating family of leaf-nosed bats, is carnivorous, and is known to eat small rodents and birds, as well as other bats. The Vampire Bat has the strangest diet of all, for it lives exclusively on the blood of other vertebrates. The incisor teeth are large and razor-sharp, and vampires can usually cut into a sleeping animal and lap its blood without awakening it.

Many of the smaller bats roost in caves by day, and in

VAMPIRE BAT

bats have small eyes, and probably poor vision. The Microchiroptera in flight send out bursts of sound so high in pitch that humans can not hear them. These sounds are reflected back to the bats as echos, and warn the bats both of obstacles and insects. The scientific name for this is "echolocation." It tells the bat both the nature and size of any object in its path, and the distance. If you have ever tried to catch a flying bat in a net you know how easily the bat avoids capture.

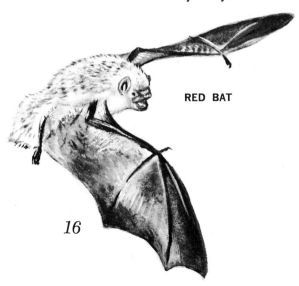

RED BAT

16

Primates

MUCH AS we might like to think that this order, to which we ourselves belong, is the most highly evolved, the fact remains that primates have changed less, physically, through time than most other mammals. As a group, though, primates are the most intelligent of mammals. The Insectivores are the ancestors of this order, and the most primitive of living primates, the Tree-Shrew, or Tupaia was for a long time thought to be an insectivore. Most primates are more or less man-like in form, but the more primitive species are not.

Tree-Shrews (TUPAIIDAE)

Tree-shrews are found in tropical Asia and some surrounding islands. The Common Tree-shrew has a squirrel-like body with a pointed snout like a true shrew. It is diurnal, lives in trees, and eats both animal and vegetable matter.

Lemurs (LEMURIDAE)

Members of this family are limited to the island of Madagascar. All have dog-like faces and monkey-like bodies. Most are nocturnal, but the Ring-tailed Lemur is active by day, and is less arboreal than the others, dwelling in rocky habitats. Although most lemurs are about the size of a house cat, several are quite small. The Dwarf Lemur and Mouse Lemur, large-eyed, and short-snouted, are the smallest of primates.

RING-TAILED LEMUR

AYE-AYE

17

TARSIER

SLENDER LORIS

Indri (INDRIIDAE)

Related to the lemurs, the four species in this family also live only on Madagascar. The Indri is an oddly marked, black and white short-tailed lemur-like creature. It is active by day, and arboreal. It may eat birds but is chiefly herbivorous. The Sifakas are more monkey-like in appearance, and like the Indri, are diurnal tree-dwellers. The Avahi, unlike the other members of the family, is nocturnal.

Aye-Aye (DAUBENTONIIDAE)

The nocturnal Aye-aye of Madagascar is so strange that it has been placed in its own family. Although related to the lemurs, it scarcely looks like a primate, and seems to have been put together from spare parts. The size of a cat, the Aye-aye is covered with coarse, grizzled fur, has large, naked, floppy ears and a long, bushy tail. Its most striking feature is its enormously long, slender fingers. The Aye-aye's rodent-like incisors are used to gnaw through wood to reach boring insects, which, along with vegetation, form its diet.

Lorises and Pottos (LORISIDAE)

The lorises of tropical Asia, and the pottos of Africa are nocturnal, arboreal creatures which eat small animals, fruits and leaves. They are slow-moving climbers. Also in this family are the galagos, very active, long-tailed primates, capable of long leaps in their treetop haunts. Like the lorises and pottos, galagos are nocturnal. The smaller species are called bushbabies.

GOLDEN MARMOSET

NIGHT MONKEY

SPIDER MONKEY

Tarsiers (TARSIIDAE)

The tarsiers of the islands off southeast Asia have the general form of bushbabies, but have larger eyes. They, too, are arboreal and nocturnal, and prey heavily upon small animals and insects.

Marmosets (CALLITHRICIDAE)

If we wanted to split hairs, we might say that marmosets are not really monkeys. For all practical purposes they are monkeys, but of an odd type. They are small New World primates, arboreal and omnivorous. They vary in color and in hair arrangement, some having bald heads and others tufts and plumes on the head. Unlike other monkeys marmosets have a flat nail on the big toe, and claws on the other toes and fingers. Marmoset fathers usually carry their young around, in contrast to other monkeys. Although it is a marmoset, the rare Callimico has some of the features of the next family.

New World Monkeys (CEBIDAE)

All of the remaining species of monkeys found in the Western Hemisphere belong to one family. Many have prehensile tails. Their hind feet are handlike. The closely related Titi and Night Monkey, or Douroucouli, look not at all alike, and the second is the only nocturnal true monkey. Among the most bizarre of monkeys are the sad-faced sakis, whose long mantles conceal the slenderness of their bodies. The uakaris have the same long hair and slight build as the sakis, but two species, the Red and the Bald Uakaris have such short, sparse hair on their

RED UAKARI

WANDEROO

COLOBUS MONKEY

heads that they seem bald. Their faces are bright scarlet, and they differ from all other New World monkeys in having short tails.

Old World Monkeys
(CERCOPITHECIDAE)

All of the monkeys of Africa and Asia belong to this single family, which includes the ground-dwelling baboons of Africa, and the almost totally arboreal leaf monkeys. Most species are limited to the tropics, but one, the Japanese Macaque, is found on the southern islands of Japan. Most of the Old World Monkeys are omnivorous, though chiefly vegetarian. The Guenons of Africa are a large group of species, all very closely related, but varying widely in color and pattern. All except the ground-dwelling Patas Monkey are arboreal, and most have brightly colored faces—some

with blue skin. The tails of these creatures are long, but not prehensile.

The leaf-eating monkeys form a separate subdivision of the family. So adapted to a diet of vegetation are they that their stomachs are compartmented like those of the cow family. The langurs are Asiatic species. The closely related colobus monkeys, or guerezas, of Africa are beautiful creatures. Most are black or black and white, but one species, the Bay Colobus, has chestnut-colored hair of many shades. The macaques are Asiatic monkeys. Most resemble the common Rhesus Monkey although the Wanderoo, with its lion's mane, is unusual.

Great Apes (PONGIDAE)

The great apes are our own closest relatives, and they are

PATAS MONKEY

20

MOUNTAIN GORILLA

CHIMPANZEE

often called Anthropoid ("man-like") Apes. They live only in the Old World tropics, the Chimpanzee and Gorilla in Africa, and the Orang-utan and gibbons in southeastern Asia and the surrounding islands. They are primarily vegetarians. All live in fam-

WHITE-HANDED GIBBON

ily groups, moving through the forests unhurriedly. As fearsome as they look, Gorillas are peaceful creatures, and can rarely be provoked to attack a man.

Much smaller than the Gorilla (although males may weigh about 200 pounds), the Chimpanzee has a wider range. A number of races are known, which vary in face

color, from pink to black. Chimps are the most intelligent of the great apes.

The Orang-utans are found on the islands of Borneo and Sumatra. They are heavy-bodied, red-haired apes, and males develop thick-skinned pads at the sides of their faces, and a flabby big pouch on the throat. The throat pouch acts as a magnifier of the Orang's roar. Orangs spend most of their time in trees. Gibbons look like tailless spider monkeys, with their long arms, but are true apes. They are master acrobats and swing effortlessly from branch to branch.

ORANG-UTAN

THREE-TOED SLOTH

"Toothless" Mammals

EDENTATES ARE among the strangest and most varied of all the orders of mammals. The name "edentate" means toothless, but most of its members do have teeth, although these are usually mere pegs of dentine. The edentates live in the New World tropics, but one species, the Nine-banded Armadillo, ranges north into the United States. Three families exist today.

Anteaters (MYRMECOPHAGIDAE)

Anteaters are the only toothless members of the order. They lap up ants and termites with their long sticky tongues and swallow them whole. The Giant Anteater has such large stout claws on its forefeet for tearing apart insect nests that it walks on its knuckles, with the claws curved backward. The other two species of the family are smaller and arboreal. The Tamandua has a prehensile tail, as does the tiny Silky, or Two-toed Anteater, as an aid in anchoring itself while opening the nests of tree-dwelling ants and termites.

Sloths (BRADYPODIDAE)

The two species of this family are built along the same lines, but differ in several features. Both have three toes on the hind feet, armed with long claws, but the Two-toed Sloth has only two toes on each forefoot. The Three-toed Sloth has three on its forefeet.

GIANT ANTEATER

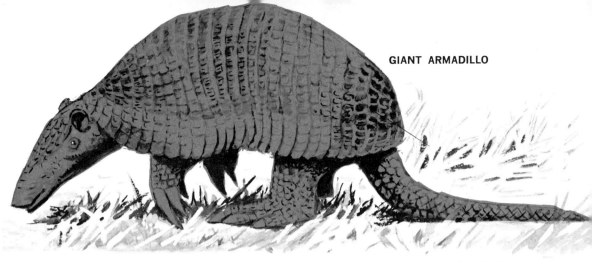

GIANT ARMADILLO

They are slow-moving vegetarians that normally rest and move hanging upside-down by their hook-like claws. The Two-toed Sloth is normally yellowish gray, but in the humid, sunny treetops algae grow on its hairs, camouflaging it with a greenish hue. The shorter haired Three-toed Sloth is known to eat only the leaves of cecropia trees.

Armadillos (DASYPODIDAE)

The dozen and a half or so species of armadillos are protected by bony plates buried in the skin on the upper surface of the body, hinged to allow for the animals' movement. Their stout claws suit them for digging. Armadillos eat insects, but some also dine on vegetable matter and carrion. They vary in size from the pig-sized Giant Armadillo of the Amazon forests to the tiny Fairy Armadillo, six inches long. Unlike other armadillos, the Fairy Armadillo's armor is attached to its body only along the spinal column, and its body, under the shield, is clothed in long silky fur. Armadillos are chiefly nocturnal.

Scaly Mammals

ALL of the species in this, the only family of the order, look alike, differing in the length of tail, and development of the external ear. The pangolins inhabit Africa and Asia. They are armored above with overlapping horny scales (not bony plates like the armadillos), but their undersides and the insides of their legs are hairy.

Pangolins protect these soft areas by rolling into a tight ball, like armadillos. They are nocturnal, and eat only ants and termites, lapping them up like the anteaters. Most pangolins are ground-dwelling, and live in burrows, but the Long-tailed Pangolin is arboreal. Pangolins are toothless.

AFRICAN PANGOLIN

BLACK-TAILED
JACK RABBIT

Rabbits
And Their
Relations

THE MEMBERS of this order were once considered to be a special type of rodent, but are now recognized as a separate order. Unlike the rodents, which have a single pair of incisor teeth in each jaw, the lagomorphs have a second, small pair in the upper jaw. Lagomorphs are found on all continents except Australia (and they have been brought there by man). All are strict vegetarians.

Rabbits and Hares
(LEPORIDAE)

Two general types of animals, each with many species, make up this family. The first, the rabbits, bear blind, naked, helpless young, while hares are born with open eyes, well furred, and able to move about.

COTTONTAIL RABBIT

Pikas (OCHOTONIDAE)

Pikas, inhabitants of the mountainous areas of North America and Asia, look like small, very short-eared rabbits, and in a sense, they are. Their habits differ from the rabbits and hares in that they live chiefly in rocky areas, and make hay for future use. Pikas lay cut grasses and herbs out to dry, taking them into the rocky recesses when it rains, and setting them out again afterward. They are diurnal.

PIKA

24

CAPYBARA

SILKY POCKET MOUSE

Gnawing Mammals

THIS ORDER has more species than any other. With so many species of rodents it is not surprising to find that they have branched out to occupy all sorts of habitats, from the hottest desert to the cold arctic tundra. Some have taken up an underground life, becoming modified for burrowing. Others are adapted for swift running, jumping, tree-dwelling, and still others for gliding through the air. Still other rodents are aquatic. There are thirty families of rodents, too many to talk about individually, and we will have space to see only a few. Notice that the various adaptations, as for example, jumping, are not confined to any one family, but are found scattered throughout the order. The fact that many jumping rodents look alike is due to their adaptation for that way of life, and has nothing to do with their relationship to one another.

The chief characteristic of all rodents lies in the number and form of their teeth. The big "buckteeth" of a squirrel or beaver are the trademark of rodents. All have a single pair of these incisor teeth in the upper and lower jaw. Canine teeth, or fangs, are lacking, and there is a wide gap between the incisors and the molars or cheek-teeth. The incisors have the shape and function of chisels, with a hard enamel layer in front and a softer layer of dentine behind. The incisors continue to grow and be worn away throughout the rodent's life, and, since the dentine wears away faster than the enamel, the incisors always retain their sharp cutting edge, enabling the rodents to gnaw through wood and nut shells.

MOUNTAIN BEAVER

FORMOSAN FLYING SQUIRREL

PREVOST'S SQUIRREL

Most rodents are about squirrel size, but a few are as big as a pig. The Silky Pocket Mouse of southwestern United States is smaller than most shrews, while the Capybara of South America, as large as a pig weighs as much as 100 lbs. Most rodents are vegetarians, but many eat flesh. The Grasshopper Mouse has largely abandoned vegetable food and preys heavily upon insects, other invertebrates, and even on small rodents. Some rodents, like the hamsters, have large cheek pouches in which they carry food to their dens.

Sewellel (APLODONTIDAE)

The Sewellel of the Pacific Northwest U.S. is the most primitive of living rodents, closely resembling its ancestors, which are the earliest known members of the order, and the ancestors of all present day rodents.

Squirrels (SCIURIDAE)

Members of the squirrel family are found throughout the world, except for Australia. Not all squirrels live in trees; some, such as the Antelope Ground Squirrel of the southwest are ground dwellers, as are the chipmunks, though both can climb trees. Even the marmots, such as the Woodchuck and Hoary Marmot are heavy bodied squirrels. Among the most strikingly colored of the squirrels is the Prevost's Squirrel of Asia. Flying squirrels represent an attempt by the rodents to conquer the air, but, like

HOARY MARMOT

CHIPMUNK

POCKET GOPHER

BANNER-TAILED KANGAROO-RAT

the Colugo, they have been only partially successful, and really glide. While most squirrels are active by day, flying squirrels are creatures of the night. In Asia some flying squirrels grow to a yard in length.

Pocket Gophers
(GEOMYIDAE)

The pocket gophers are found only in North and Central America, but they have independently evolved counterparts elsewhere. The forefeet are armed with long claws used in digging. These animals, too, have cheek pouches of large size used to carry food. Where gophers are common the landscape is filled with piles of earth from excavated tunnels.

Pocket Mice
(HETEROMYIDAE)

Pocket mice and their cousins all have cheek pouches. The largest members of the family are the kangaroo rats. Like most jumping mammals they move on all four feet except when in a hurry. Most of the pocket mouse family are desert dwellers. When desert plants form seeds these little rodents spend most of their waking hours gathering and storing them underground, to be eaten when food is scarce. Heteromyids can live without water to drink, for they manufacture it within their bodies from the starch in the seeds they eat.

BEAVER

Beavers (CASTORIDAE)

The beavers, more than any animal except man, have changed the face of the Earth. The dams they built across streams have formed ponds and caused changes in local vegetation. The value of beaver fur led trappers into the wilderness of North America in the early days of our country and brought about much of the early exploration of this continent.

GRASSHOPPER MOUSE

BUSHY-TAILED PACK-RAT

Hamster Family (CRICETIDAE)

One of the largest families of rodents, the cricetids abound on all continents except Australia.

The family is named for the European Hamster, a large cousin of the Golden Hamster. The dens of some species of packrats, made of sticks, and as much as six feet high, are conspicuous features of the landscape in parts of North America. The white-footed mice and Grasshopper Mouse are also members of this family.

A subdivision of the cricetids are the voles and their relatives, stocky, short-tailed mice, for the most part. The Pine Mouse is a woodland species, but most voles live in open grassy habitats. The largest vole is the aquatic Muskrat, a web-footed, long-tailed marsh dweller. The cheek teeth of voles, like their incisors, grow continually, to counteract the abrasive effect of the grasses on which they feed.

Springhaas (PEDETIDAE)

The Springhaas of South Africa is the only species of its family. It is nocturnal and lives by day in a burrow. It resembles a large jerboa, and moves in much the same way.

PINE MOUSE

Old World Mice (MURIDAE)

This is one of the largest families of rodents, but oddly enough most of its members closely resemble one another. They are not native to the New World, but occur naturally on all other continents, including Australia. The House Mouse and Norway and Black Rats are the best known members of this family, which have followed man around the world in his ships and have become established wherever humans live.

Not all murids are pests, and many species are clean, beautiful creatures. The Spiny Mouse of the Middle East has the hairs of its back modified into stiff spiny bristles. The 3 foot long Giant Pouched Rat of Africa is one of very few murids with cheek pouches. It has the unusual habit of inflating these pouches with air when it is excited, making its head seem to double in width. Most of the remaining species are very plain rats and mice, but a few, like the Striped Mouse are handsome, striking animals.

Jumping Mice (ZAPODIDAE)

Another family that has mastered the art of leaping has species in North America, Europe, Asia and Africa. All are small mice with

EGYPTIAN JERBOA

large hind feet and very long tails. The Woodland Jumping Mouse of North America hibernates underground in the winter.

Jerboas (DIPODIDAE)

The Jerboas of the Old World deserts are counterparts of the kangaroo rats and have similar habits.

SPINY MOUSE

AFRICAN CRESTED PORCUPINE

Old World Porcupines (HISTRICIDAE)

The largest of the porcupines belong to this family, which ranges through Africa, Europe and Asia. The Crested Porcupine is a large rodent with fewer but larger quills than the New World types. The Brush-tailed Porcupine of Africa is small, and more slender than the others. Like the New World porcupines, the members of this family are most active at night.

New World Porcupines (ERETHIZONTIDAE)

The members of this family are chiefly arboreal, and like the Old World species, are strict vegetarians. The Coendu, of South America, uses its prehensile tail, tightly wrapped around branches, as an aid in climbing.

30

Cavies (CAVIIDAE)

In this small family are the cavies, one of which is the creature from which the various multi-colored and long and short haired breeds of domestic Guinea Pig have been derived. Originally native to the Andes Mountains of South America, Guinea Pigs were domesticated centuries ago by the Inca Indians. The rabbit-like Patagonian Cavy of the South American pampas runs with a peculiar bounding motion.

Capybara (HYDROCHOERIDAE)

This family contains only one species. The Capybara of the South American tropics, is seldom found far from water. The largest of rodents, it is a strict vegetarian.

Pacarana (DINOMYIDAE)

Forming another family with but a single species, the Pacarana burrows, and is a plant-eater, like the Woodchuck of North America.

PATAGONIAN CAVY

SPERM WHALE

Whales and Porpoises

T HE CETACEANS are mammals that have totally given up life on land, and most of them are so adapted to an aquatic existence that they soon die if stranded on a beach. The whales and porpoises are large, virtually hairless mammals whose aquatic life has produced widespread changes in body form and habits. Cetaceans have large, paddle-shaped forelimbs, and have lost all external traces of hind limbs. Their tails are broad and horizontally flattened. Their nostrils are located high on the top of their heads. One species, the Blue Whale, is the largest animal of any kind that ever lived.

Toothed Whales

River Dolphins (PLATANISTIDAE)

Small, fresh water porpoises, found in tropical rivers of South America and Asia. The Ganges Dolphin lives in waters so muddy that its eyes, useless in this habitat, have degenerated. Like many other porpoises it locates the crayfish and other slow aquatic species on which it feeds by echolocation.

NARWHAL

84481

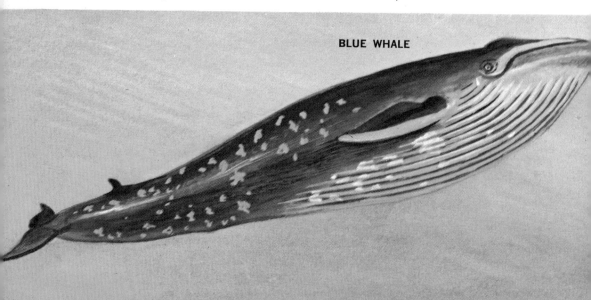

RIGHT WHALE

Sperm Whales
(PHYSETERIDAE)

The Sperm Whale is the largest of the toothed whales reaching a length of 60 feet (the Pigmy Sperm Whale is less than 13 feet long and belongs to this family, too). Sperm whales have many peg-like teeth. They eat a variety of marine creatures, including huge squid, which they hunt at depths of over a thousand feet at times.

Narwhal and Beluga
(MONODONTIDAE)

The Beluga, or White Whale and the Narwhal, both of the northern oceans, make up this family. The Narwhal has only a single tooth, located in the upper jaw. It is very small in females, but in males grows out as a spirally-grooved tusk up to nine feet long.

Dolphin (DELPHINIDAE)

Most of the small dolphins, or porpoises belong in this family. They are playful, highly intelligent creatures. The savage Killer Whales, scourge of seals and other whales, belong here, too. Roaming the seas in packs, Killers, up to 30 feet long are the most feared inhabitants of the oceans.

Porpoises (PHOCAENIDAE)

These are small cetaceans, seldom exceeding six feet in length. They are similar to the dolphins in form (except for their blunt snouts) and habits.

BLUE WHALE

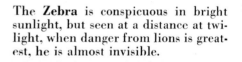

The **Clouded Leopard's** spots and blotches make him seem part of the branch on which he generally lies in wait for his prey in the forest.

WAYS of LIFE

Animals are remarkably fitted for the ways in which they live. Their colors and patterns help to hide them from the animals they hunt — or which hunt them. Their shapes and habits are suited to their roles in life, and they have developed a variety of means of attack and defense. Provided with the same senses we have, different species have refined and increased their use of one sense or another, according to their needs.

These things did not happen intentionally. Nature has tried many experiments, and we see only those that worked. The failures died off and were not carried on to future generations. Here are some of the successes:

This **Whitetail Deer** fawn's spots blend with the woodland's patchy sunlight. He will lose this camouflage when he is big enough to defend himself.

The **Zebra** is conspicuous in bright sunlight, but seen at a distance at twilight, when danger from lions is greatest, he is almost invisible.

FEET

The **California Sea Lion's** mobile flippers allow him to move quite well on land, but they are best adapted for movement in the water.

An **Otter's** feet are webbed for swimming, but the webs fold out of the way when he is on land, and he uses his feet as well as any land mammal.

The **Whitetail Deer** walks upon its toe-nails, which are enlarged into hoofs. The feet themselves do not touch the ground.

A **Polar Bear's** entire foot, from nails to heel, touches the ground in walking, to support his great weight.

The **Lion's** foot, like others adapted for speedy travel, carries weight only on the toes, with the rest of the foot clear of the ground.

LIFE UNDERGROUND

The **Allegheny Packrat**, approaching her young in the nest, spends most of her life in the darkness of a cave, but must come above ground daily to find food.

SENSES

A **Fennec's** huge ears serve two functions — acute hearing and efficient loss of excess body heat (from their great surface area), a necessity for a desert animal.

The **Florida Packrat,** like most rodents, holds its long whiskers aimed forward when running, to warn him, by touch, of obstacles in his path.

The **Coati's** sensitive nose tells him of insects and other small creatures hiding out of sight.

A **Bushbaby** can see very well at night in the dark forest. Like the Bushbaby, most nocturnal mammals have large eyes.

The **Black-shouldered Opossum** of Peru is one of the rarest of mammals. The function of its color pattern is not known.

Only male **Mandrills** have this bright facial coloring. Bright colors are found only in monkeys, for they would be useless to other mammals, which are color-blind.

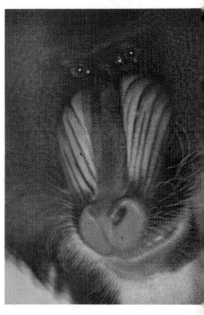

Jaguarundis, because of their two color phases, were once thought to belong to two distinct species. Actually, both colors may be found in the same litter of kittens.

Nyala antelope show great differences in appearance between the sexes. How many differences can you see between the male and the female standing in front of him?

DEFENSE

The **Muskox** makes use of his sharp, curved horns to protect himself and his calves from his chief enemy, the wolf.

The **Pangolin** is covered by overlapping horny scales. When attacked he rolls into a ball to protect his soft underside.

The **Canada Porcupine** defends himself with his sharp, barbed quills. This one is presenting his prickly back and tail, as he would to an attacker.

Bighorn Sheep

Caribou

Rhinoceros

Giraffe

TYPES OF HORNS AND ANTLERS

The antlers of this **Caribou**, as of all deer, are made of solid bone, growing from the skull. They are shed and re-grown annually. While growing they are covered with hairy skin and are said to be "in velvet."

The **Giraffe's** "horns" are really short antlers permanently "in velvet," and never shed.

The **Pronghorn Antelope** is unusual in that it sheds its horns annually and regrows them over their permanent bony core.

The horn of a **Rhinoceros** is a solid mass with no bony core or connection with the skull. It grows continuously.

The "horn" of a **Narwhal** is not a horn at all, but a greatly elongated tooth.

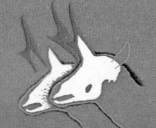

The **Bison** and **Bighorn Sheep,** like other bovids, have true horns which grow continuously over a bony core. The horns are unbranched, and are never shed.

SKIN   BONE   HORN   HAIR

LIFE IN THE WATER

Bottle-nosed Dolphins, like other whales, are the most perfectly aquatic of mammals, and never leave the water. Still, they are air-breathers and must surface regularly.

The **Harp Seal** is clumsy on land, and easy prey for Polar Bears. In the water it is graceful and speedy.

The **River Otter** spends only a part of its time in the water. It is perfectly at home on land and normally takes the fish it catches ashore to eat.

Whalebone Whales

THESE ARE whales without teeth. Instead, they have huge, frayed plates of baleen, or whalebone, growing from the roof of the mouth, which are used to strain small marine invertebrates (krill) from the water. Even the Blue Whale lives on these creatures, which are usually no larger than shrimps.

KILLER WHALE

BOTTLENOSE DOLPHIN

Finbacks (BALAENOPTERIDAE)

This family contains the largest of all animals, the Blue Whale, which may measure 100 feet or more in length, and weigh up to 150 tons. All species have plaited throats, which can expand to take in large quantities of krill-laden water. The Finback looks like a smaller edition of the Blue Whale.

Right Whales (BALAENIDAE)

These large-headed whales have unplaited throats and lack dorsal fins. They are large (up to 70 feet), thick-set whales. The Bowhead and Right Whales make up the family. The Right Whales were named because their dead bodies floated and were easier for whalers to get at, making them the "right" whales to hunt.

FENNEC

Meat Eaters

T HE CARNIVORES are primarily flesh-eaters, but many are omnivorous, and a few are totally vegetarian. Their incisor teeth are small. The canine teeth are enlarged into fangs used in biting their prey, and the cheek teeth are modified for cutting, grinding, or both.

Dogs (CANIDAE)

All members of this family, from the Maned Wolf to the tiny Fennec, or Desert Fox, are easily recognized as dogs, and, in fact,

BUSH DOG

there are fewer external differences between the wild canids than between the breeds of the single species of domestic dog. All wild canids have long pointed snouts and more or less bushy tails. They occur all over the world. The Dingo, of Australia, is not native to that continent, but was brought there by the first humans, thousands of years ago.

The foxes are small canids recognizable by their prominent

ears and sharply pointed muzzles. The Bush Dog of South America is a short-legged, short-eared dog that has a bird-like voice.

Although the teeth of dogs are adapted chiefly to a diet of meat, most, if not all species eat large amounts of fruit and other plant material as well.

Bears (URSIDAE)

Bears are large, heavy-bodied members of the order Carnivora which have become omnivorous, even more so than the dogs, to which they are related. The Brown Bears of the Northern Hemisphere are the largest land-

MANED WOLF

living carnivores in the world. The Spectacled Bear, with its peculiar facial markings, is the only bear native to South America. It is a creature of the mountains. The Polar Bear of the Arctic is partly aquatic and can be seen swimming far from land. It travels often on ice floes, and during the arctic winter lives chiefly on seals. Asia is the home of three other species of bears, the Sloth Bear, the short-haired Sun Bear of the tropics and the shaggy Himalayan Black Bear of the higher regions.

Raccoon Family
(PROCYONIDAE)

ALASKAN BROWN BEAR

The members of the raccoon family are so different in shape that if it were not for their internal anatomy you might find it hard to believe them related. While they are carnivores and do eat living animals, all of the species dine extensively on fruit and vegetable matter, perhaps even more so than their close relatives, the bears. All but 2 species are found in the New World. The Crab-eating Raccoon of Central and South America has short hair, which grows forward rather than backward over the neck. The Cacomistle preys heavily upon small vertebrates but will not pass up fruit. The least raccoon-like member of the family is the Kinkajou, or Honey Bear. It is arboreal and much more of a vegetarian than other procyonids. Its tail is prehensile. The last spe-cies, the Olingo, looks like a Kinkajou with the pointed snout of a Cacomistle. Its tail is not prehensile and is slightly more bushy than a Kinkajou's, and sometimes has faint light and dark rings.

Of the two Asiatic members of the family, the Lesser Panda is the more raccoon-like externally. The Giant Panda, on the other hand looks like an oddly marked

POLAR BEAR

bear. It feeds almost entirely on bamboo shoots, and like the Lesser Panda is a mountain dweller.

GIANT PANDA

Weasels (MUSTELIDAE)

Members of the weasel family differ greatly in appearance and habits. Mustelids are found on all continents except Australia, but are most numerous in the temperate zones. The weasels and some other species are strictly carnivorous, while others, the skunks, for example, eat almost anything. The smallest mustelid

is the Least Weasel, only six inches long. The seven foot long **Giant Otter** is the largest. Badgers are heavy-bodied creatures with stout-clawed forefeet useful in burrowing. The European Badger, unlike the not-too-closely related American species is omnivorous. All members of the weasel family have scent glands capable of emitting a strong odor, but the skunks have perfected these glands as a means of defense, and can spray their contents several feet with accuracy. Skunks are restricted to the New World, the Striped and the smaller Spotted Skunks living in North America

Civet Family (VIVERRIDAE)

The viverrids, of Africa, Asia and Europe are in many ways counterparts of the weasel family. They are basically predators, but many eat non-animal food as well. The best known species of this family is the Indian Mongoose, which has an over-rated reputation as a cobra killer. A native of tropical Asia, it eats a variety of small vertebrates. It was introduced into Hawaii and the West Indies many years ago in the

LEAST WEASEL

erroneous hope that it would control rats and snakes. Instead, it took a heavy toll of poultry and wild birds and became a serious pest. The Banded Mongoose of East Africa is a small, burrow-dwelling creature of social habits. There are many other species of mongoose which differ in habits and appearance. The Black-footed Mongoose of Africa has a doggy look; Meerkats live in colonies like prairie dogs, and have a perpetual quizzical expression.

INDIAN MONGOOSE

The civets are small to medium sized creatures with cat-like habits. They are primarily carnivorous. One of the most unusual of the civets is the Binturong of southeastern Asia. Bear-like, with a long, prehensile tail, it is arboreal, nocturnal and omnivorous. The Genets of Africa and southwestern Europe are long-bodied relatives of the civets.

Hyenas (HYAENIDAE)

The hyena family of Africa and Asia contains few species, most of them carrion feeders, with

GENET

powerful jaws capable of cracking bones with ease. Most hyenas will kill small animals but rely heavily on the kills of other carnivores. While hyenas look like dogs, they are more closely related to the civet family. One odd species, the Aard-wolf, looks like a small hyena with a hairy crest along its back. Its weak, small teeth can handle carrion, but termites form the bulk of its diet.

Cats (FELIDAE)

The members of the cat family are far more restricted to a meat diet than most other carnivores. Cats inhabit all of the land areas of the world except Australia. All but the Cheetah have claws that retract into sheathes in the toes to prevent wear in walking, for their claws are used to slash prey. Most cats are active on and off during both day and night. The Lion once in-

SPOTTED HYENA

TIGER

habited a good part of Asia as well as Africa, but for centuries its Asiatic range has dwindled, and only a few remain in part of India. Lions are animals of open, grassy areas, and unlike other cats, live in groups, called prides. The Tiger inhabits forested regions from the Indian tropics to Siberia. Like most mammals, the northern Tigers are larger and more heavily furred. The Leopard of the African and Asiatic tropics is primarily a forest animal, agile enough to carry its kill into a tree. Black panthers, a color phase of the Leopard, are sometimes found in Asia. Smaller than the Leopard, but larger-looking because of its thick fur, the Snow Leopard, a distinct species, is found high in the mountains of central Asia. The deep tropical forests of southern Asia are the haunts of the beautiful Clouded Leopard, a long-tailed cat with large squarish blotches, and proportionately the longest fangs of any cat. Only two species of large cat inhabit the Western Hemisphere, the Jaguar of the tropics (occasionally found in extreme southwestern United States) and the Puma, which ranges from Canada to southern South America, in a wider variety of habitats. The Cheetah, of Africa and Asia, has a dog-like body and limbs, adapted for running speed. It is said to run as fast as 70 miles per hour in short spurts. While its usual speed may not be this high, it is the fastest of mammals, and easily runs down antelope.

Various species of smaller cats occur throughout most of the world, and one or more species can usually be found from the inhospitable deserts to the Arctic Circle. Some, like the Golden Cat of Asia and the Caracal of Africa have plain, yellowish coats. The Jaguarundi of tropical America, the most nocturnal of the cats, may be either reddish or gray in color.

CHEETAH

Pinnipeds

O NCE CONSIDERED to form a separate order, the seals are now thought to be a subdivision of the Carnivora. The pinnipeds fall into 3 families, which differ slightly in their adaptations to an aquatic life. All are carnivorous, and obtain their food in the sea. The four limbs are modified into flippers.

Earless Seals (PHOCIDAE)

FUR SEAL

The animals in this family lack external ears. They do not use their hind feet in moving about on land, but do use them for propulsion in the water. The teeth of seals are generally sharp and scissor-like, to hold and kill fish, which are swallowed whole as a rule. Most of the earless seals are ocean-dwellers, but one species is found in fresh water. Male Elephant Seals exceed fifteen feet in length, and have an inflatable tapir-like snout.

WALRUS

Fur Seals (OTARIIDAE)

This is the first of the two families of eared seals, and contains the Sea Lions, Sea Bears and Fur Seals. They can support themselves with their hind feet as well as the forefeet, and use both in moving on land. In the water they propel themselves chiefly with the front flippers. All are oceanic.

Walrus (ODOBAENIDAE)

The Walrus, of the Arctic seas is a heavy-bodied, nearly hairless seal. Its canine teeth are modified into tusks, which are used in fighting and to rake up the ocean floor in search of the molluscs and starfish on which it feeds. The remaining teeth are heavy, broad grinders, designed to cope with the shells of its food.

Aardvark (ORYCTEROPODIDAE)

The Aardvark, because of its many peculiar characteristics, has been placed in a family and order of its own. The origins and relationship of this creature to other groups of mammals are almost unknown, and it has at times been thought to be related to the pangolins, and to the edentates, although neither group is now considered to be closely related to it. The name Aardvark is Afrikaans meaning "earth pig", and the animal does resemble a pig at first glance. It is pig-sized, and has a pig-like face, but there the

AARDVARK

AFRICAN BUSH ELEPHANT

resemblance ends, for the Aard-vark has peg-like teeth and eats termites and ants, which it laps up with its long anteater's tongue. It is nocturnal and spends the day asleep in its burrow.

Elephants (ELEPHANTIDAE)

Elephants are found today in Africa and tropical Asia. Two species occur in Africa, the Bush Elephant, largest living land mammal, and the smaller Forest Elephant. The Forest Elephant, limited to the west central part of the continent stands only about seven feet high, and has smaller, more rounded ears. A big male Bush Elephant stands over ten feet tall and weighs over five tons.

The Asiatic Elephant is not as large as the African Bush Elephant, and is quite a different animal, with small ears and a more arched back. It has been used as a beast of burden by man for centuries, but has never truly been domesticated.

The elephant's trunk is one of the most unusual organs of any mammal. With its trunk an elephant can grasp objects, and siphon up water to be squirted over itself for bathing or into its mouth to drink. The trunk is actually an elongated, muscular nose. Elephants' tusks, largest in

ASIATIC ELEPHANT

males, are greatly elongated incisor teeth. Elephants are strict vegetarians.

Hyraxes (PROCAVIIDAE)

Strange little rodent-like creatures, the hyraxes are actually close relatives of the hoofed mammals. Their feet bear small, claw-like hooves, and hyrax teeth resemble those of the rhinoceroses. The Tree Hyrax is an arboreal forest dweller, but the remaining species live on the ground in rocky areas. The hyraxes are chiefly vegetarian.

Sea Cows

O NLY TWO families exist today, the manatees of the New World and the dugongs of the Old World. Both have blunt faces and porpoise-like tails. Both have paddle-shaped front flippers, and lack hind legs. They are totally aquatic and herbivorous, and limited to tropical waters. Manatees have recently been imported to inland lakes in the tropics in the hope that they will reduce the aquatic vegetation that menaces boat travel. Manatees have rounded tails; the dugong's is forked like a porpoise's.

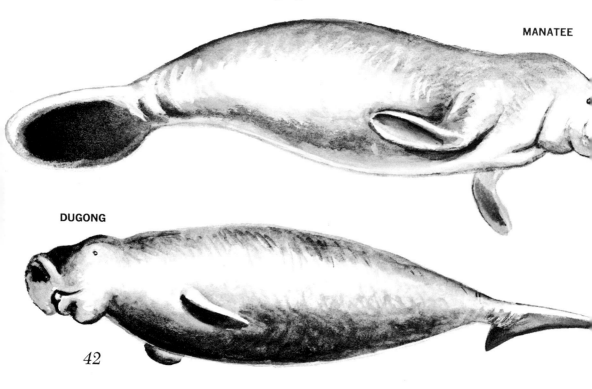

MANATEE

DUGONG

RZEWALSKY'S
'ILD HORSE

GRANT'S ZEBRA

Hoofed Mammals

THERE ARE today two orders of hoofed mammals, one in which the species have an even number of toes on each foot, and the other in which an odd number of toes are found. In both orders the toes end in hooves, which are greatly enlarged nails, broadened to support the weight of the animal, so that the foot itself is totally free of the ground. All hoofed mammals are vegetarians, but a few, the pigs, are omnivorous.

Odd-Toed Mammals

Horses (EQUIDAE)

In this, the first of the three present-day families of a once great order, only a few kinds of animals remain, all very closely related and very similar in form, and all now limited to Africa and Asia. Only one species of true wild horse exists today, the Mon-

MALAY TAPIR

golian, or Przewalsky's Wild Horse, once common throughout Asia and Europe, but now restricted to a small area in Mongolia. Several kinds of wild asses, or donkeys live in Africa and Asia. One of these, the Onager, looks more like a horse than a donkey. The remaining wild horses are the zebras, all African. Although zebras are conspicuous in zoos, their stripes make them difficult to see at a distance on the grassy African plains. In the horse family, reduction of toes has reached its peak, and only one toe remains on each foot.

Tapirs (TAPIRIDAE)

In prehistoric times tapirs were found over most of the world, but today they live only in the New World tropics and in southeastern Asia. Tapirs are heavy-bodied forest-dwellers with odd, flexible, elongated snouts. Their feet bear short, stout hooves, four on each front foot and three on each hind foot. They are herbivorous. The young are striped and spotted, unlike their uniformly colored parents. Differing in color and pattern from the New World tapirs, the Malay Tapir is a blackish species with a light, saddle-like patch.

Rhinoceroses
(RHINOCEROTIDAE)

The rhino family of Africa and Asia contains several species, the remnants of a group that once ranged as far north as Europe during the Ice Age. Rhinos are large, heavy-bodied creatures (the White Rhino is second in size only to the elephants). The skin of rhinos is extremely thick, and in some species is folded into armor-like shields.

WHITE RHINOCEROS

Even-Toed Mammals

Pigs (SUIDAE)

MEMBERS OF the pig family occur in Africa, Asia and Europe. Pigs are omnivorous, with teeth able to chew a variety of foods. In some species the canine teeth have become grotesque tusks, used for rooting in the earth, and fighting. The almost hairless Babirusa of the East Indies has its upper tusks growing up through the skin of its snout; these are found only in males, and are probably more for decoration than usefulness.

Peccaries (TAYASSUIDAE)

Similar to the true pigs in appearance and habits, the peccaries of North and South America differ from them in enough ways to form a separate family of their own. They live in small bands, which when aroused can put even the largest predator to flight. Peccaries have a prominent odorous gland on the back.

BABIRUSA

Hippopotamuses (HIPPOPOTAMIDAE)

Two very distinct species of hippopotamuses, both limited to

PECCARY

DROMEDARY

Africa, make up this family. Hippos are totally herbivorous. The Nile Hippo has a wider range, throughout most of the watercourses of the continent. It is more aquatic than its smaller cousin, and its eyes and nostrils are raised slightly above the top of its head, allowing it to see, and breathe, while otherwise completely submerged. Adult males weigh two tons or more. Nile Hippos often congregate in large herds in sluggish rivers.

Camels (CAMELIDAE)

Another family whose ancestors occupied much of the world in past ages, but is limited today to South America and Asia is the camel family. Most of the members of the family have been domesticated and used by man as beasts of burden, sources of wool and food for centuries. Only the Old World members, the camels, have humps, which are large deposits of fat that vary in size with the nutritional state of the animal. The Dromedary, or One-humped Camel is a native of the Middle East, but has been transported and used by man in desert areas throughout the world. The camel's broad hooves are well suited for travel over loose sand. The Bactrian Camel of northern Asia has two humps and a longer shaggier coat. It, too, has been domesticated since early times.

LLAMA

46

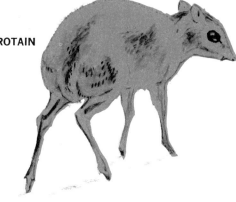

In the temperate regions of South America two species of this family live. The New World camelids are smaller than camels and more gracefully built. The Vicuña, smaller of the two, inhabits the high Andes. The second species, the Guanaco, is larger, and is found both in the mountains and on the plateaus.

From the Guanaco, two domesticated breeds have been produced. The Llama is a sturdy animal used for centuries by the Indians of the region for food, wool and transport. The Alpaca has an extremely long, shaggy coat.

MOOSE

Chevrotains (TRAGULIDAE)

The chevrotains are small, deer-like animals most closely related, in a distant way, to the pigs and camels. They are generally brownish, with light spots and streaks. All inhabit dense forests in Africa and southern Asia.

Deer (CERVIDAE)

The many members of this family occur in Asia, Europe, North and South America. The males have antlers, which differ from the horns of the cow family in that they are composed solely of bone, are branched, and are

AXIS DEER

as the males of the Reindeer and Caribou carry them. The young of many deer are spotted, but lose their markings as they grow older.

Giraffe and Okapi (GIRAFFIDAE)

Only two kinds of animals, the Giraffe and the Okapi, form this family. Strange as it may seem the towering Giraffe has in its long neck the same number of bones, seven, as most other mammals. Giraffes are animals of the plains, and their long necks are useful in browsing trees. The Giraffe is well adapted for this method of feeding, but must bend its forelegs awkwardly to drink from a waterhole. There are five races of Giraffes, but many interbreed and there are intermediate forms. Despite its ungainly ap-

shed entirely and regrown annually. Not all deer are large. The Muntjac and Water Deer of Asia are no bigger than small dogs, while the Moose of North America, Europe and Asia are the largest. Antlers take many forms, from the broad, flat spreading type of the Moose to small, singly branched spikes of the Muntjac. The Water Deer lacks Antlers entirely, while the females, as well

REINDEER

GIRAFFE

OKAPI

pearance, the Giraffe can run rapidly. Males may stand 17 feet or more high at the head. All Giraffes have a pair of short horns permanently covered by the skin of the head; some races have a third horn in front of the pair.

The Okapi was one of the last large mammals to be discovered. Until 1901 it lived unknown in the Congo forests, until a naturalist saw an ornament made of a strip of skin from an Okapi's leg. He thought it had come from an unknown forest-dwelling zebra. Instead, the Okapi proved to be a far stranger animal, of much more scientific in-

terest than a zebra would have been. For the Okapi is a forest-living relative of the Giraffe. It is not surprising that the Okapi remained undiscovered so long, for its habitat is so dense that the animals can hear a man coming long before he could come close enough to see them. Only the males have horns, similar to a Giraffe's. Both Giraffes and Okapis have long, prehensile tongues used to grasp leaves that are otherwise out of reach.

Pronghorn (ANTILOCAPRIDAE)

There is only one living species in this family, the Pronghorn "Antelope" of North America.

PRONGHORN

BIGHORN SHEEP

Although they look like antelopes, Pronghorns are unique creatures. Their horns differ from those of the antelopes in two ways: they are branched, and the horny outer covering is shed every year, leaving the bony core, which grows a new sheath. The horns of true antelopes are never shed, and are never forked. Pronghorns are prairie animals, and scattered members of a herd signal one another by erecting the white hairs of their rumps, producing a flashing effect that is visible over long distances.

Cow Family (BOVIDAE)

It must seem peculiar that the many different-seeming kinds of mammals that we will see next are placed in this one family. You may think it is easy to tell cattle, goats, sheep and antelopes apart. Under the skin they are all very much alike, though, and there are a number of species that bridge the gaps between these groups, and which cannot easily be classified as either sheep, goats, cattle, or antelopes. Except for some antelopes, in which the females lack horns, both sexes have horns made up of a bony core growing out of the skull, and covered with a continually growing sheath of horn. Horns are usually larger in

CAPE BUFFALO

males, and take many shapes, depending upon the species. All members of the family are vegetarians. Wild cattle are found throughout the world, except Australia. Two species of true buffalos (not bison) are found in Africa. The Cape Buffalo is a large open-country dweller, while the small, reddish Forest Buffalo prefers the dense tropical forest growths. A small Asiatic species, the Anoa, lives in the forests of a few islands off Southeast Asia.

The wild sheep are characterized by massive coiled horns, particularly in the rams. Most are similar in general appearance.

Asia and Europe is the home of the goats, sure-footed inhabitants of rocky, mountainous areas. Some have short, simple horns, while others are adorned with intricately sculptured or twisted horns. Males of all antelopes bear unbranched horns on their heads, which may be greatly twisted, spiralled and curved. In some species the females, too, have horns. Antelopes range in size from the huge Eland, as big as a cow, down to the tiny Dik-diks and Royal Antelope, which are not much larger than a rabbit. Only a few antelope such as the Bongo and several small species called Duikers are found in the

GREATER KUDU

51

forests, and most antelopes occur in the open grassy plains, where we find the greatest variety and numbers. Antelope differ greatly in shape. Some, like the White-tailed and the White-bearded Gnus, are angular and blocky in build; others like the Kudus and Nyala are deer-like.

Goat-like animals, differing from the true goats anatomically are the Goat-Antelopes, denizens of the steep rocky mountainsides of North America, Europe and Asia. Two of the best known species are the Rocky Mountain Goat and the Chamois. Both species live in small groups, and the young, when only a few days old, can follow their mothers over the precarious trails of their habitat.

Two other species which look more like cattle than the goats, to which they are more closely related are the Musk-ox and the Takin. Both are large, heavy-bodied creatures of the northern

ROCKY MOUNTAIN GOAT

regions. The Takin, of north-western Asia is a mountain dweller, found in the vast rhododendron forests. Although it appears clumsy, its broad hooves and balancing ability allow it to climb steep slopes easily. The western form is a grayish color, but those from China are a rich golden yellow.

TAKIN

INDEX